Brought to you by J GOSPEL

Dedicated to

LORD JESUS CHRIST

FOREWORD

Children of this generation are bombarded by distractions. Electronic and interactive devices have captivated their minds. Traditional Bible study groups may no longer retain the full interest of our youth.

I resigned as Pastor from a church and started J Gospel Net Inc. in 2006 to bring forth the Gospel and advance God's kingdom through Internet ministry. Especially for children born in this era, we want to bring them a fun way of learning words of God.

This graphic book (which also comes in e-book and app version) is designed for children between ages 6-12. It is a perfect material for children's Sunday school. By using this book, teachers can discuss with the children religious and everyday topics. It can also serve as a children's bedtime story that builds a bridge between parents and their children. Parents can provide guidance to children as they grow up through a story they both share.

We thank Lord for providing us with a team of talented and dedicated workers. May the Lord bless you and keep you.

Sincerely,
Rev. Roycos Hom
Founder of J Gospel Net Inc.

One day, God told Jonah, "Go, and talk about me to the people of Nineveh." But Jonah gave a big, resounding "No!"

Jonah didn't like the Ninevites! So, instead of doing what God asked him to do, he ran away and boarded a ship headed in the opposite direction.

Suddenly, a great wind started blowing on the sea.

All the sailors were really scared by that big storm, and they were all crying out to their own gods.

...all except for Jonah, for he knew very well for whom the storm was.

The sailors called Jonah saying, "Jonah, why aren't you praying?" So Jonah explained, "Because I am running away from my God."

The rest of the crew was terrified, "What have you done?!" they asked. "How can we make the sea calm down for us now?"

Jonah knew the answer. "Pick me up and throw me into the sea," he replied.

The sailors hesitated but they couldn't see any other option. Jonah had to leave their boat.

As soon as they threw him out, the storm stopped. The men were in awe and started praying to God.

As for Jonah, God sent an enormous fish to swallow him whole.

Jonah lived in the fish's belly for three days and three nights - plenty of time for him to think and to realize that he was wrong. So he prayed and asked God for forgiveness.

God heard Jonah's prayer and commanded the fish to spit him up, safe and sound, on a beach.

Once again, God said to him, "Go, and talk about me to the people of Nineveh." This time Jonah said, "Yes!"

Once at Nineveh, the shipwrecked, fishy-smelling Jonah gave the Ninevites God's message, "In forty more days Nineveh will be destroyed." Everyone believed him and was very worried.

Jonah couldn't believe his eyes - every single person in the city started repenting for their bad behavior, and to show God how sorry they were, they wore sackcloth and they didn't eat or drink for days.

God saw their hearts and decided to forgive them.

But this made Jonah mad! He didn't like the people from Nineveh and he didn't feel like they deserved God's compassion.

So he decided to cool off by sitting outside the city walls. God arranged for a tall, leafy plant to grow above his head and give him shelter from the sun.

But the following morning, a little worm chewed its way through the plant, which withered and died. The blazing sun was shining in the sky and a scorching wind came, leaving Jonah hot and bothered.

"I'm so angry!" shouted Jonah, "I wish I were dead!"

But God patiently replied, "Jonah, you are angry about losing the plant, even though you didn't grow it yourself. How much more should I be upset to lose all the people and all the animals of the great city of Nineveh?"

God wanted Jonah to realize how absurd it was to care more for a plant than for all the people of Nineveh. Jonah's hatred had made him blind!

Suddenly it all made sense. God not only was at work in the Ninevites' lives, He was at work in Jonah's life too.

Copyright © 2018 by J Gospel Net Inc.

All rights reserved. No part of this book may be used or reproduced in any manner whatsoever, without written permission except in the case of brief quotations embodied in critical articles and reviews.

Paperback First Edition ISBN: 978-1-62931-034-3

Written by Rev. Roycos Hom.

Translated by Laura Caputo-Wickham.

Illustrated by Yuling Deng.

First printing edition 2018.

J Gospel Net Inc.
22 Howard Street, Bsmt C,
New York, NY 10013 USA

www.jgospel.com

www.ingramcontent.com/pod-product-compliance
Lightning Source LLC
Chambersburg PA
CBHW040025050426

42452CB00003B/142